Hungry
Dinosaurs

Dr. Alvin Granowsky

STECK-VAUGHN
L I B R A R Y
A Division of Steck-Vaughn Company

**Illustrations by
Carol Inouye**

Look at all of these dinosaurs.

Did you know there were so many dinosaurs?

Many dinosaurs had flat teeth.
Flat teeth are good for cutting
and chewing plants.

4

Their flat teeth show that these dinosaurs
were plant-eaters.

Look at these little dinosaurs.
The smallest ones were the size
of a greyhound dog.

Did you know that some dinosaurs
were that little?
These little dinosaurs were plant-eaters.
You can tell by their flat teeth.

Brachiosaurs were not little dinosaurs.
They were the biggest animals that ever
walked on land.

They were so big the ground shook
when they walked.
These big dinosaurs were plant-eaters.

The big Apatosaurus could eat the leaves
of very tall trees.
Like other plant-eaters, it had flat teeth.

The Camptosaurus ate the leaves
of smaller trees.
The Stegosaurus ate low-growing plants.

Look at the teeth of this Allosaurus.

Its teeth are very sharp.

A Velociraptor had sharp teeth, too.
Sharp teeth are for eating meat.

13

Can you see the sharp teeth
on these meat-eaters?

14

Look at the little Dromaeosaurus dinosaurs.
Look at the big Tyrannosaurus.
They all have sharp teeth.
Can you guess what kind of food they ate?

We know that dinosaurs with flat teeth
ate the leaves of plants.
Do you know what this dinosaur ate?
IT ATE OTHER DINOSAURS!

When an Allosaurus was hungry,
it went looking for meat.

17

Where would an Allosaurus find food?

If it was lucky, the Allosaurus might find
a baby Brachiosaurus that had moved away
from its mother.

It took a lot of food to fill up a hungry Allosaurus.
A baby Brachiosaurus would make a good meal
for an Allosaurus.

20

A baby dinosaur had no way to protect itself.
A fierce Allosaurus could easily win a fight
with a baby Brachiosaurus.

But scientists believe that some adult dinosaurs
may have protected their babies.
A mother Brachiosaurus might come
to help her baby if she heard it crying.

Other Brachiosaurus might come
to help fight the Allosaurus.

Scientists believe that several Allosaurus together
might attack a dinosaur as large
as an adult Brachiosaurus.
But one Allosaurus by itself
might not have been so brave.

24

A grown Brachiosaurus weighed
more than ten elephants.
If a big Brachiosaurus stepped on an Allosaurus,
the Allosaurus would be crushed!

An Allosaurus would not attack
so many big dinosaurs.

26

It would probably go away and look somewhere else for food.

An Allosaurus would keep hunting
until it found food.
It could walk many miles
on its big, strong legs.

Plant-eaters such as a Camptosaurus
were not safe when an Allosaurus was hungry.
The teeth and jaws of a plant-eater
were not suited to fighting.

But an Allosaurus had sharp teeth and claws.
Its jaws were powerful.

30

A Camptosaurus could only survive
by running away!

But sometimes a dinosaur could not escape.
Sometimes, the hungry Allosaurus found a meal.

Look for these animals in
▬ Hungry Dinosaurs ▬

Allosaurus
(al uh SAWR uhs)
1, **12**, 12, **16-18**, 17-21, **20**,
23-26, **24**, **27-30**, 28-30, **32**, 32

Dromaeosaurus
(droh mee oh SAWR uhs)
15, 15

Tarbosaurus
(TAHR buh sawr uhs)
14

Ankylosaurus
(an KY luh sawr uhs)
3

Heterodontosaurus
(het uhr uh dahn tuh SAWR uhs)
6-7

Triceratops
(try SEHR uh tahps)
2

Apatosaurus
(a pat uh SAWR uhs)
1, **3**, **10**, 10

Iguanodon
(ih GWAN uh dahn)
3

Tyrannosaurus
(tih ran uh SAWR uhs)
3, **15**, 15

Brachiosaurus
(brak ee uh SAWR uhs)
8-9, 8, **19**, 19-25, **21-23**, **25-26**

Maiasaura
(my uh SAWR uh)
2

Ultrasaurus
(uhl truh SAWR uhs)
5

Camptosaurus
(kamp tuh SAWR uhs)
3, **4**, **11**, 11, **29**, 29, **31**, 31, **32**

Stegosaurus
(stehg uh SAWR uhs)
3, **5**, **11**, 11

Velociraptor
(vuh lahs uh RAP tawr)
3, **13**, 13, **14**

Boldface type indicates that the animal appears in an illustration.

Acknowledgments
Design and Production: Design Five, N.Y.
Illustrations: Carol Inouye
Line Art: John Harrison

Staff Credits
Executive Editor: Elizabeth Strauss
Project Editor: Becky Ward
Project Manager: Sharon Golden

Library of Congress Cataloging-in-Publication Data

Granowsky, Alvin, 1936–
   Hungry dinosaurs / written by Alvin Granowsky: illustrated by Carol Inouye.
     p. cm.—(World of dinosaurs)
   Summary: Describes a variety of herbivorous and carnivorous dinosaurs, including the Brachiosaur and Allosaurus.
   ISBN 0-8114-3252-1
   1. Dinosaurs—Juvenile literature. 2. Herbivores, Fossil—Juvenile literature.
3. Carnivora, Fossil—Juvenile literature. [1. Dinosaurs.] I. Inouye, Carol, ill. II. Title.
III. Series.
QE862.D5G733   1992
567.9'1—dc20   91-23405
                                                     CIP AC

1 2 3 4 5 6 7 8 9 LB 96 95 94 93 92